THE NEW YOU

THE NEW YOU

A Handbook on Etiquette and Personality Development

RAGHURAM MARAYATH

PARTRIDGE
A Penguin Random House Company

To order additional copies of this book, contact
Partridge India
000 800 10062 62
www.partridgepublishing.com/india
orders.india@partridgepublishing.com

Contents

Preface

There are several habits and practices, both acquired from family and outside, through exposure to the world, in various journeys undertaken by modern mankind and through learning from friends. The changes that are taking place around us are so fast that either one does not get wind of it or is ignorant and oblivious to these happenings, so one does not take cognizance of them. They simply do not interest us or we are not bothered about what goes on around us . . . One sticks to the lessons and manners learnt from one's young age without even a fleeting thought as to whether it is right or not. The basic human ego "I am Right" comes into play most often. Many times one faces embarrassing moments in a crowd, among friends, in office, in front of a girlfriend or boyfriend as the case may be or in a meeting.

This book is an attempt to teach willing learners, both the old and the young, a lesson or two, through interesting episodes, to improve their personality and confidence, their personal presentation, their conversational abilities and overall to be a better human being with a sense of better understanding and care for others. This book will largely help the young men and women who have not had a public school background and who are afraid of asking others for help on various etiquettes, for fear of being ridiculed by the so called modern society. While this book could serve as a ready reckoner of some sort there maybe many more areas one needs to probe and learn for complete personality development.

I hope this earnest attempt brings out a new and a better "you" who can be a proud asset to our nation, to your family, friends and colleagues, besides being perfect ambassadors both within the home and outside.

I take this opportunity to thank my wife, Meena, who has been the only person who encouraged me in my maiden endeavor. I also must thank a few friends who corrected me whenever I made a mistake. I had made a mental note of these which helped me in writing this book. Let me also thank Vinuta Nalcoor for contributing the illustrations and Anjali Ramesh for doing the final editing.

If there is anything in this book that might hurt the sentiments of some readers, it is purely accidental. Examples have been given only to prove a point.

The Author

The Smart Family

Brigadier Chellatil Ambat Thulsidas Menon, was often fondly called CAT Menon by his friends and colleagues. This nick name stuck. He was a smart Army Officer who has been decorated with several bravery medals during the Kargil war (with Pakistan) and also in fighting Maoists in the Darjeeling District of West Bengal. He was also honored as the Best Dressed Officer in many an Army Officers' party. He was a handsome man, towering at 6' 3". He took pride in dressing up well every morning while going to office so much so that he spent a long time in front of the mirror. His wife used to chide him often and CAT Menon would ignore these comments which helped in keeping out confrontations.

His wife, Kamala, was from a very rich family in Kochi, but not very cultured from his point of view. This resulted in arguments often, especially when they had to attend formal parties with his Commanding Officer as well as whenever they played hosts. She was indeed beautiful and carried herself pretty well. She had that sway of hips that made her look quite sexy. Menon was well aware of that. However, she did not bother to dress formally but was rather casual . . .

They had two grown up children, a son, Rohit, aged 23 years and a daughter, Arti, aged 20 years. It was a very happy family always light hearted and joyful. CAT Menon hailed from a town called Trichur in Central Kerala. Trichur, as you might know, is considered to be among the 'top 5 humorous districts' in the world. Almost everybody who belongs to Trichur have a mischievous smile most of the time. This invariably translated into subtleness in their everyday conversations, sometimes having dual meanings. One had to be watchful and careful while speaking to shopkeepers especially so as not to be caught on the wrong foot that might embarrass you unless one is either thick skinned or ignorant.

Most of the early part of CAT Menon's career was spent with the family except when he had to serve in the border areas. Although he would have quarters in the peace zone when he was serving in the border areas, his wife chose to stay in Kochi so as not to disturb the children's studies. Kochi is a cosmopolitan city with good schools. Most of the students in these schools had their parents in the Middle East who would come visiting once or twice a year. CAT Menon's wife stayed with the children during their formative years in school and once they were into high school she moved in with her husband only to return during their final years in school and 2 years of their Pre university so that they remained focused on their studies. Both of them were good at studies. Rohit wanted to be a Mechanical Engineer while Arti wanted to get into advertising. Both had completed their education, Rohit, BE in Mechanical Engineering and Arti, BA in English Literature. They had applied to a few companies and were awaiting interview calls. "One thing that was lacking in the children, was polish, although they were both well behaved" thought CAT Menon. They were very casual in their dressing like their mother. Menon, as you know, was quite finicky in his dressing as he was from the Army background.

Rohit was now a qualified mechanical engineer and was receiving interview calls from various software companies. That day was a Saturday and he had gone out with a friend for an old Hindi movie and was scheduled to come home for lunch. His father CAT Menon had gone to buy seer fish which was the family's favorite. A couple of slices of fried fish along with rice, sambar *(a vegetarian dish made for lunch in most south Indian homes),* a dish of boiled vegetables, mango pickles, pappadam (as papad is called in Malayalam (a south Indian language), banana chips followed by payasam, a mouthwatering dessert made up the main menu. Ice creams summed up this rather sumptuous lunch. It was quite a spread.

Arti was busy helping her mother prepare lunch in the kitchen. She was also interested in experimenting new recipes of dishes. That day she was trying out baked fish with cheese. Although this was a European dish she wanted to try it out and in case it was a disaster she would not mind as there were adequate backup dishes. Mrs. Menon ensured that their daughter learnt to cook well so that she wouldn't be at sea in the kitchen after she got married.

After CAT Menon got back from shopping he looked forward to a glass of chilled beer along with Rohit and Arti, before lunch. His wife would join him for an occasional Vodka and orange juice This was a very cosmopolitan family with a broad outlook to life. CAT Menon knew the values of life. Being on the front lines as an Army Officer he has had quite a few close shaves with life. He therefore wanted to enjoy life to the fullest as long as he was alive.

Finally, lunch was ready and Arti was laying the table. CAT Menon was closely watching how she was going about it. He was a stickler for table manners and wanted his family to follow this strictly so that they would never feel out of place anywhere.

"Hey, Hey! Hey . . . . Kamala, let Arti lay the lunch table. Let's see what she has learnt." said CAT Menon.

"That is a great idea. Arti, I am sure you would do a wonderful job." said Kamala, Arti's mother.

"Umm! Why do you pick on me always?" cried Arti.

"Come on, Arti" said Rohit. "Take this as a challenge and prove how adept you are at this ".

"OK!. I'll do it but promise me you will not laugh at me if I make a mistake." said Arti subtly.

"Done, but we would correct you so that you would learn." said her father.

"So, here we go" announced Rohit.

"1, 2, 3 . . . Start," said her father.

Meantime, Kamala hurriedly prepared a soup (Rasam).

First came the full plates and then the quarter plates (also called side plates) which were kept to the left of lunch (full) plates. A fork was kept to the left hand side of the full plate. A table spoon and a knife were placed on the right hand side of the full plates. On the full plates was kept a soup spoon and a dessert spoon. On the side plate (*quarter plate*) was kept a small towel. Four such sets were arranged and the lunch table was laid. Arti had taken special care to ensure that all the items were neatly in place and it gave a fabulous appeal, not to forget, a ravishing appetite.

"Excellent" exclaimed CAT Menon. "That's my daughter for you. I am beginning to feel really hungry. A neatly laid table makes a world of a difference."

"So are we." said the others in chorus.

It was a buffet lunch, so the dishes were placed on a table in the far side of the dining room to make it convenient for all to take whatever they wanted. Brig CAT Menon led the team. He walked across to take soup in the soup bowl that was kept adjacent to it on the table. He walked back to his favorite chair and sat down. He waited till the others joined him at the table. It is good manners to wait for others to be seated before you start eating.

After all had sat down he said "Let us start".

First, they put the table napkin or serviette *(as it is also called)* on their lap to ensure that they did not spill any food on their dress.

They took the soup spoon and after tasting the soup they added salt or pepper as required.

Following this one by one they went to the food table and picked up the serving spoon that was kept in a plate in front of the food bowl and helped themselves with the food into their plate. Whenever they wanted a second helping they went to the food table and after helping themselves they returned to the dining table. After they had sat down CAT Menon said "Let me tell you one more thing. In between your meal you might go back to the food table to help yourself with some more of your favorite dish. While doing so please ensure that you do not use your right hand to take chapattis or rotis or papads, or for that matter even the spoons kept in the food bowls, from the food table to put them in your plate because during the course of your meal you might have used this hand to touch your food in your plate like biting your chicken leg or for something else. Although you might have used your towel to wipe your hand it is not considered hygienic and proper to touch the food on the food table with your right hand. Many have this habit which must be scrupulously avoided."

From the corner of his eyes he saw his wife taking the dessert spoon and holding it in her right hand and holding the knife with her left hand. None of them are left handed in the family. He saw his son following suit.

 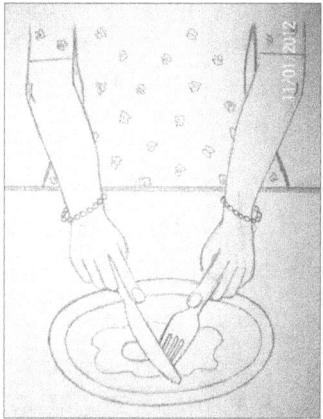

"Just a second." he said. "Have you forgotten how to use your fork, spoon and knife? Kamala, you are holding the dessert spoon instead of the table spoon. On your left hand one has to hold the fork and the knife in your right hand as it is easier to slice or cut the piece of chicken or mutton with that hand. The piece is then pierced using the fork with the knife supporting it and eaten, "just like this." he demonstrated. "If you are not using the knife but only the fork and spoon, hold the fork in your left hand and the table spoon in your right hand and use your fork to push the food onto the spoon, like this." he demonstrated again. After you take a helping and are chewing your food, please keep the fork and spoon back on your plate. Do not let it swish in your hand as you are talking or chewing. At no time, while eating, should your hands rest on the table."

Rohit quickly changed the dessert spoon to a table spoon in his right hand lest his father would comment again.

"By the way, Arti, your baked fish and cheese is excellent" praised her father.

"Let me narrate to you an incident I witnessed while having lunch at one of the posh restaurants-Barbeque Nation—in Indiranagar" continued CAT Menon. "There was this girl and a boy, obviously from one of the software companies close by, in their mid twenties, having lunch at the next table. To start with they were novices at the use of table cutlery . . . . knife in the left hand and fork in the right. I was curious as to how she was managing to eat. Sure enough suddenly I heard a muffled yeeeohhh!!!. While she was eating, she was talking at the same time swishing her knife with her left hand and suddenly it hit her face on the side when she let out that howl. Luckily it did not hurt her much. There was just a small cut." said CAT Menon concluding his story.

"You must practice this time and again so as not to embarrass yourself or the people around you." repeated CAT Menon. "At home, within your four walls it is fine, but if you do not make this your second nature you tend to make mistakes time and again. Secondly, you must eat as silently as possible. Always chew food with your lips closed. Do not look like a cow chewing the cud.

Avoid talking with food in your mouth. If you need to belch suddenly, do it as silently as possible and ask to be excused instead of roaring like a lion and drawing the attention of everybody around you. Similarly, when you cough please ensure you cover your mouth with your handkerchief to avoid spreading any infection. Once you have finished your meal place your eating cutlery neatly vertically on your plate. This is an indication to the steward in the restaurant to clear the table. At home you must drop the waste in the kitchen waste basket and keep the empty plate in the kitchen sink after rinsing so that they don't dry up and start stinking before they are washed later."

"Dad," said Rohit. "Can I ask you a question?"

"Go ahead" said CAT Menon.

"We are all Indians and most of us are all used to eating with our hands. Why can't we follow this instead of aping the West?" remarked Rohit.

"According to the Puranas or Ancient scriptures eating with your fingers are allowed provided the food you eat does not go beyond the first digit of your fingers at all times. If anyone can do that they are welcome. Licking your fingers is not allowed as it is considered rude and uncouth. The plate or leaf *(in South India people eat from a banana leaf on auspicious occasions)* should be clean at all times. In western countries people have started using their hands to eat. However, they are careful not to spill the food or keep their fingers dirty. They would always wipe it after eating hamburgers, Kentucky fried chicken, tandoori chicken, etc." This ended the conversation.

After lunch, each of them carried their dessert into the drawing room and enjoyed it while relaxing and watching the T20 cricket match played between Chennai Super Kings and Mumbai Indians.

All of a sudden the doorbell rang.

"Arti, please see who is at the door." yelled Rohit on top of the excitement on the television. Chennai Super Kings had just lost a wicket.

"It's the courier. There is one for you and one for me as well." Arti exclaimed.

"Who could that be from?" muttered Rohit as he made his way to the front door.

In one voice or so it seemed, both Rohit and Arti yelled "I have been called for an interview."

"Me too. Mine is on Monday" said Rohit excitedly.

"Mine is on Wednesday" said Arti equally excited. "It's from NDTV for the position of a Trainee editor."

"Mine is from Infosys. Don't know the position but it sure excites me" Rohit exclaimed. "I need to do some shopping, Dad. I want to buy a new shirt and a pair of socks for the interview. Can I borrow one of your neckties?" asked Rohit.

"Sure, why not we have early tea and go out shopping, say around 5 in the evening?" suggested CAT Menon.

"Arti, please also check if you also require anything for the interview. We can finish the shopping and perhaps have dinner at the Taj." announced CAT Menon. "Let me get 40 winks before that so that I feel freshened up."

After tea the entire family got ready to go out shopping to Commercial Street, the business hub of Bangalore where CAT Menon was currently posted. While they were driving from their home in Koramangala CAT Menon asked Rohit what he planned to wear for the interview.

"I have light grey trousers which fit well. I thought of wearing a dark blue shirt and one of your red striped ties with a pair of blue colored socks and brown shoes." replied Rohit.

"Son, I thought some of my good tastes and sense of dressing would have rubbed off on you. I am indeed disappointed." said CAT Menon. A giggle was heard from the back seat. Arti was muffling a hearty laugh.

"Please remember that a formal suit means a pair of dark trousers, preferably plain, a jacket of the same material and color, a white shirt preferably or any pastel shades like light sky blue, light cream or light green full sleeved shirt, a pair of laced shoes and a matching pair of socks. Have you ever noticed any European/ American / Japanese/ Chinese businessman or for that matter any Indian executive wearing any other shirt other than a white shirt or any shirt of a pastel shade with a dark suit? You can then wear striped or checked or a plain coloured necktie. If you wear a striped or a checked shirt the suit loses its elegance. It is not appropriate to wear different shades of trousers and jacket for interviews".

"Anyway, I will buy you a pair of dark blue or a grey trousers, a white shirt, and a pair of plain blue socks. You can use my dark blue striped tie. You have to wear black shoes and a matching pair of socks. Rohit, educational qualification alone is not adequate to create a good impression when you meet your interviewers. A smartly dressed clean shaven or with a well trimmed moustache and well groomed hair would be ideal. A smart young man oozing with confidence, who can deliver, is what they are looking for. I hope you know how to put on a tie. They know your background from the CV you have sent. Now, what they are looking for is to confirm their impressions after meeting you besides gauging your integrity and honesty. So answer all questions honestly. Do not try to hoodwink them. They are too smart for you and can see through you instantly. Always knock at the door and ask if you may come in before entering the room for the interview. Please sit only after you have been offered a seat and say a polite 'Thank You' after sitting down. Do not slouch on the chair or sit uncomfortably stiff. It is also bad manners to sit with one leg crossed over the other. Just be relaxed and have a smile on your face always.

"Now coming to Arti, you too have an interview on Wednesday. Do you have a proper dress to wear for the interview?" asked her father.

"Yes, Dad. I have a new pair of jeans you bought me the other day. I could wear a white top and a pair of well heeled sandals" said Arti. "After all in this industry of journalism people wear casual clothes as they have to go different places to cover different events," she continued after a slight pause.

"You must be out of your mind to even think of wearing such a dress for an interview even though, as you say, jeans and T shirt are acceptable in this industry." said CAT Menon raising his voice a little. "Remember, you have to first create a good impression at the interview and also do well so as to get the job. Casually attired could mean that an element of seriousness is lacking. That is why it is very important that you are dressed neatly and groomed well. Let me tell you something. Most Indian companies prefer their female staff or managers to wear a saree and blouse or an elegant salwaar suit. This goes with Indian culture. Some western companies who have their offices in India do not mind their female staff wearing western clothes.

Let me narrate to you a story. One of our distant relatives' daughter was called for an interview with Lufthansa, the German airlines, in Mumbai for the position of Flight Stewardess. About 40 women attended the interview that day. To her utter disbelief all of them except her were dressed in western clothes while this girl was dressed in an elegant silk saree. She did look very attractive in it though, she thought *"that was it,"* but decided to attend the interview for the sake of experience. She was one of the last to be called. She noticed that none of the others called earlier were selected because she saw all of them come out of the interview crestfallen. When this girl's turn came for the interview she walked in boldly knowing she wasn't going to make it and hence had nothing to lose. Her interview lasted 10 minutes and she was selected. The panel members said they were looking for an Indian woman sporting an Indian attire so that she could give a homely feeling to the passengers on the flight. She later learnt that she was the only one selected that day by Lufthansa Airlines.

As for you, I would suggest you wear a good saree with a matching blouse. It would look elegant. Let us do the shopping now as there may not be time if we miss today".

They walked down Commercial Street until they found a good retail outlet which looked well stocked with the latest varieties of dresses, as also with the fashionable ones. Arti did not take much time in choosing a good simple yet glamorous saree. It suited her very well and she looked smart. CAT Menon's wife was looking around at some sarees when her husband suggested to her to buy one if she liked. She chose a plain dark blue chiffon saree which looked very elegant. It came with a blouse piece and lining which saved her the effort of searching for a matching blouse piece.

That's when Arti suggested to her dad to buy a shirt and a trouser for himself. "No" he said. "I have enough and more to last me for the next 5 years."

"That's a laugh." joined in Mrs Menon. After a lot of persuasion Brig CAT Menon said he would look at a plain lemon colored shirt. He did not have to spend much time in finding the exact shade he wanted.

Finally, having completed all the shopping they drove to Taj Residency on M G Road and parked the car in the portico. They had earlier put all their shopping into the car boot so as not to attract any attention when the car was parked in the car park outside by the hotel valet. They then walked into the restaurant for a well earned meal. They did not realize how famished they were and were looking forward to enjoying their dinner.

Daddy CAT Menon said he would have a Johnny Walker Black Label Whisky with water and ice and Mrs Menon asked for a Bloody Mary (Vodka and tomato juice). Arti asked for a lemon juice with ice and soda. When the steward walked towards Rohit he looked up at his dad who was giving him a soft glare. Immediately, Rohit understood. He was the driver for the night and alcohol was forbidden for him. They had not brought their official driver, a bad decision in retrospect. The traffic police were on the prowl to book errant drivers who had consumed alcohol. So he ordered a lemon juice with ice and soda. While the drinks were being served, the family decided on their dinner menu and placed their order when the steward came along. Brig Menon ordered for a couple more large whiskies while the others decided to have soup instead. After all he could sit back and enjoy the drive back home. He was not going to be at the wheels.

As they were waiting for dinner to be served suddenly CAT Menon broke the silence by enquiring "By the way, have any of you attended any group discussions during your college days? Well this is a very important part of an interview process. This is done to judge the candidates' maturity, confidence and knowledge. Let me tell you briefly.

Group Discussion (GD) is an inevitable part and parcel of interviews.

What the interviewer is looking for from candidates are the following:

- Confidence
- Leadership Qualities
- Knowledge
- Ability to listen
- The ability to command and
- Team work
- All these are important in any aspect of life, particularly to become a successful Manager. While these may be lacking among freshers, an iota of your abilities will be exposed during such a GD. So it is vital that you are a good listener first, so as to get a grasp of the topic being discussed. You should keep an eye and an ear to see who is talking and if there is anything that you could contribute to add value to the discussion.

- Speaking first or all together is not the criteria. It is how you can make others listen to your point of view and thereafter discuss, with you leading it *(the discussion)*. Please remember that the time allotted maybe only five minutes and therefore you cannot afford to wait for too long to start. Please ensure that you state only facts. Otherwise a smart listener would floor you and then you are out for the count."

Dinner was served in the next 15 minutes or so followed by a loud silence as they were all enjoying their meal.

"Enjoying the food, I guess," said Rohit looking around the table. "Dad, you look tired. Yeah! Coming to think of it, yes it has been a very hard day for a weekend."

Finally, Brig Menon said "Rohit and Arti, Today your mother and I feel really proud of you. Our strict discipline and advice on etiquette have made both of you ready to face the world. We have done our duty as parents having given you a good life and good education. We will miss you when you go to your own homes after you get married". Mrs Menon and Arti could feel their eyes welling up so also Brig Menon and Rohit. They never expected Brig CAT Menon to give such an emotional touch at the end of such a busy day. In fact CAT Menon was surprised at it himself. It was a very natural feeling.

Thanks to the dim lighting inside the car the family members could not see each others' tears.

"It is almost midnight. I am looking forward to a night's good sleep" chipped in CAT Menon. "Hope we do not have visitors tomorrow. I plan to be in bed the entire morning. Rohit, you had better start preparing for your interview which is on Monday. Please get up by eight at least and read the newspaper thoroughly. You never know what kind of questions they might ask you." For the next 20 minutes or so they drove in silence. When they reached home Rohit tapped Arti to wake her up so that she would open the gate to their house by which time the security came in running to open the gate. As soon as they entered the house they all cried as if in chorus "Good Night and Sweet Dreams."

Morning came and one by one the family woke up by 7 and walked into the dining room to have their coffee and biscuits. They had a maid who would come in every morning and make their bed coffee and breakfast and at times their lunch too if Mrs Menon had some other engagements to attend to in the mornings. She would help out in the dinner preparation early and would then go home by 7 pm at the latest unless there was a party at home when her husband would also come along and help in cleaning up the place and do some last minute shopping. Mrs Menon was always the chef and she loved cooking for her family.

That day they were in for a surprise, an unpleasant one at that, considering the tough Saturday they all had. A visit from their relatives was not on the cards at all.

Around nine in the morning the silence in the house was broken by the shrill loud ring of the telephone which was kept in the anteroom next to the hall so that it could be heard right across the house and the echo making it sound louder than it actually was. Each one was waiting for the other to pick up the phone. Finally it was CAT Menon who picked it up. His wife had also reached for the phone by then.

"Hello." he growled. "Yes, this is Brig Menon. May I know to whom am I speaking to?" Through the corner of her eyes Mrs Menon could see a sudden rush of blood onto her husband's face followed by a crest fallen look.

"Hello Sandhya! How are you? How are your husband Ravi and your two sons? I forget their names . . . . Yes . . . Raj and Dilip."

"Yes, we would be very much at home unless your sister needs to go out shopping. I'll give it to her". Mrs Sandhya Nair and their family lived near Yelahanka, the other side of town. Brig Menon's brother in law worked in a private firm in Yelahanka. He was reasonably well off. They had built a two-bed roomed independent house there some 12 years ago. These days the land prices have shot up sky high. They were frequent visitors, thrice a month at least. This time they had not come for over a month since the kids were unwell with cold and fever. Subsequently, Ravi had also fallen sick. They have all since recovered and decided to come over that weekend. They would be staying on for lunch and would go back only after tea.

Brig CAT Menon sat down on the sofa with a big heave. "There goes our quiet Sunday." he exclaimed.

Mrs Menon also had a worried look on her face. She had to prepare a little elaborate lunch. After all it was her younger sister and family visiting them. The sons were very mischievous and would run all over the house. They wouldn't sit in one place. Rohit and Arti would have to be behind them all the time. After playing out in the garden they would come right in and plonk themselves on the sofa with their feet up. It was Rohit's duty to ensure that the kids washed their feet after playing in the garden before they walked into the drawing room. The last time that happened CAT Menon was left with no option but to take the kids to the bathroom himself and have their feet washed. "After all they are kids" would comment their mother. Brig Menon had other ideas. He took this opportunity to tell their parents how to teach them some discipline. Their parents wouldn't say anything until Brig CAT Menon gave the kids a tough look.

Mrs Menon would sometimes take the initiative to tell the kids to behave themselves. After all they were her nephews.

"Rohit, Arti." called out their father. "I want both of you out here in a minute. We are going to have some monsters for lunch. Please keep all your valuables safely lest they get misplaced and then don't blame anyone if something is missing."

In a jiffy they were out of their beds and started keeping their things safely locked up in their cupboards.

"Come on. How can you be so nasty with the kids. They won't take anything away." cried Mrs Menon.

"I know" howled Brig Menon. "This is only a precaution not that they would take anything away but they could have a look at our things and misplace them. We would have to search for them later on. By the way, please put sheets on the sofas and the Diwan. I don't want those kids keeping their filthy feet on them. Can't the parents teach them how to behave when they go out? They must be taught to behave at home first. Have you seen how shoddy and filthy they keep their drawing room?

(The incorrect way to sit.)

Whenever we go there I want to run away as soon as possible. How can they live in such a pigsty?"

"It's not your house, is it? Don't bother what they do. It's their business." said Mrs Menon with a scowl.

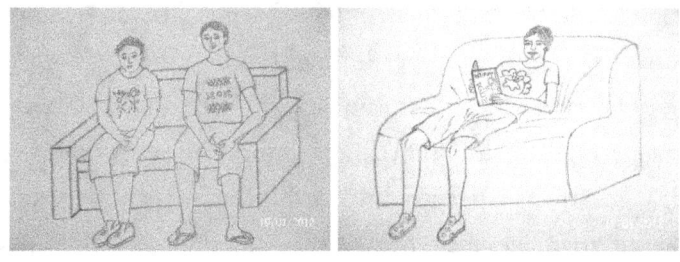

(The proper way to sit.)

"Look Rohit. Let's do one thing. From the magazine on etiquette which you'll find on the shelf, please locate some of the illustrations they have printed on how to sit on a sofa, etc. Go out and take a couple of photocopies and bring them home and leave it on the center table along with the magazines and the newspapers. When they leaf through the papers they will find it and take a look. I am sure they would learn a lesson or two without anyone teaching them and the parents would be extra cautious with their children. That is the only way out." said Brig CAT Menon.

"Don't be mean," said Mrs Menon, though in her mind she appreciated her husband's idea. She was so glad that her husband was quite tough with their children, whenever they did something wrong. Together they had brought them up with impeccable manners. They were taught to make their bed as soon as they got up. They were habituated to use their toilet as soon as they got up, brush their teeth and then have their tea or coffee. They have to be well groomed when they came to the dining table. They were even taught to clean their toilet and wash basin and keep them spotlessly clean. When they came back from school, they had to have a wash, a change of clothes before they came in for tea. They would put their used clothes in the laundry bin and not let it lie around. Both the children were fond of games and they used to play after school in the school grounds itself. They would have a lime juice with salt from the school canteen before they started for home. By this time their father would have returned from work and followed the same routine as his children. They would sit in front of the television for a while or read some magazines or chit chat for a while before they went in to study for one hour by which time dinner would be ready. After dinner Arti would help her mama clear the table and wash the dishes before she retires to bed. Mrs Menon would finish her routine before closing her kitchen for the night. She would keep a bowl of fruits on the dining table before she went in for a bath and retire to bed. Her husband would follow suit soon after.

Finally, the appointed hour came and their guests landed around 12 noon, just in time for a beer and lunch. Things went on smoothly and the children were quiet for some time. It was as if there was a calm before a storm. Lunch was taken rather quietly followed by dessert. Right through this period normal conversation was taking place. The tension was building in CAT Menon's mind and then it happened. One of the boys had spotted a cricket bat and a ball which was in the corner of the drawing room. Rohit had left it there on Friday evening and had forgotten to take it to his room. At the same time the other brother had also spotted them. Everybody's eyes suddenly moved towards the ball and before anyone could say Jack Robinson one of the boys took the bat while the other took the ball and threw at his brother. A wild swish and the ball first hit the ceiling fan, bounced back onto the center table and then went flying towards the television and rebounded to hit CAT Menon. That was it. Ravi, Sandhya and the kids quickly apologized and ran to their car before CAT Menon could react. Mrs Menon had held her husband's hand to keep him under control. Turning red on his face Brig Menon decided to cool off with a siesta. "Thank God!" exclaimed Mrs Menon and she went about clearing the lunch table and the kitchen sink which was full.

Home etiquette

"**A**rti and Rohit! Please come over. Kamala, would you also join us, please?" said Brig Menon.

"I guess today has been a day of learning along with some practical examples. At the cost of repetition let me talk to you on the etiquette to be followed at home. I am not being a Hitler but it is for your own good." continued Brig Menon.

"At the end of the day, before you go to bed please ensure that the drawing room is cleaned up. Clear the mess, if any and ensure that all the cushions are in place. Let me tell you, your mother and I learnt this the hard way. I do not want you to go through all that."

"One of the most common habits of people is to put up their feet up on the sofa and many a time with their shoes on as you saw today. It is okay if it is your house and there is no one around except your family members. However, it must be noted that this habit tends to be carried outside your homes too. It is bad manners to put your feet up on your sofa when there are others around or if you are in somebody else's house. The parents must avoid doing this and must also teach their children not to do this at home, so that when they go visiting with you or by themselves, they do not do this. Many a time one finds the children putting up their feet up on the sofa and that too with their shoes on, dirtying the sofas, as it happened today. There are situations when adults also do this. Don't you care for your friends' or your relatives' property? What right do you have to do this? To add insult to injury, many parents say "after all they are children" and do not tell them to remove their shoes. This is even worse. They forget that it is not their sofa. Would they allow their sofa to be treated like that when the kids come visiting to their houses?

It is good manners and also patience and the desire not to hurt the feelings of the guests that the host does not complain, keeping their feelings to themselves. However, you can bet, they would be silently cursing you and your kids till you leave.

Besides this, there are many other areas of concern. Keeping the toilet neat and dry, keeping the kitchen clean, etc. While these can be categorized under hygiene and cleanliness, it is essential to follow these simple factors to lead a disciplined and systematic life. Moreover, it becomes very handy when one travels abroad and stays there for some time. In the US and Europe it is very expensive to hire a domestic help. Invariably one has to clean one's own house and toilets. Washing clothes, cooking food, making your bed, etc would have to be done by you. At home, making your bed as soon as you get out of it is a sign of good upbringing. Putting away clothes that are to be washed in a laundry basket instead of throwing them all over the place and keeping your footwear clean and neatly arranged adds to the glamour in your room. Wouldn't you like to come to a neat and clean room after a day's hard work? Would it not be a welcome sight rather than entering a shoddy dirty room? Many say that they do not have the time to do all these chores. What they do not realize is that they are bad time managers. In today's world, where both the husband and wife have to work to lead a good comfortable life, it is essential that the chores are shared between all the members of the family to avoid skirmishes and unpleasantness at home. Students who have stayed in hostels are more independent than the ones who stay at home. I stayed away from home for the first time when I was transferred to New Delhi. I was brought up in a family which was not so orthodox. I learnt to do many a thing all by myself. I used to be independent at home and my mother used to teach me the household chores as she said it would come in handy at some time. How prophetic she was! However, I did not have a clue about cooking. The first time I tried my hand at cooking was when I boiled milk on an electric stove. I did not realize that the stove would remain hot even after switching it off. When I came back a little later I found most of the milk had spilt as the coil was hot and I was left with just a wee bit. One lesson learnt. We learn through mistakes and if one does not learn even after committing a mistake then life would become difficult." finally concluded Brig Menon.

Outside Home and Civic Sense

The next evening Brig CAT Menon called his family together after dinner and said "Having spoken fairly in depth last night about home etiquette, let me take half an hour of your time to explain how you should be outside your home and you should be aware of the civic sense."

"Many Indians have a tendency to spit on the roads every now and then. This not only dirties the roads but is also a very bad habit, besides causing infections to which you yourself could fall victim. The same Indians, when they travel abroad, particularly Singapore, do not spit on the road because you get punished there by the police. In India, that is not the case. It is up to the individual to ensure that spitting is avoided when they are outside their homes. Do not litter the roads. Use the waste bins that are placed on the roadside or drop them in your waste bin when you return home.

"Quite a few housemaids have the typical habit of dumping the garbage in front of their neighbor's house.

The neighbors' housemaids dump their garbage in front of their neighbor's house. In other words, in front of your house. This leads to quarrels and brickbats besides making a mess of the roadside and your gate front. Why all this? Watching from a distance it is amusing. A Sunday morning entertainment. The result, sour taste—literally— is left behind, not to forget the foul smell and the dirt. I love to live in clean surroundings. Don't you!

"Having spoken about civic sense in brief, it is important that these are inculcated first in yourself before teaching your children. You would realize this when you grow up and have kids of your own!" continued Brig Menon.

"In a super market counter, one often comes across a customer thrusting his or her hand over the heads of others saying that he is purchasing only a couple of items and therefore is demanding the right to quick disposal, jumping the queue, which is bad manners. This would apply at all places.

If only he /she excuses himself or herself and requests the others in the queue to permit him to quickly pay and go, I am sure there would hardly be any objections. Instead, they choose to be arrogant and demanding." said Brig Menon pausing to take a sip of water.

"Mumbai, is perhaps the only city in India, where you would find disciplined people waiting in a queue at bus-stops. A few years ago I was waiting at a bus-stop in Mumbai for a friend. I did not realize people were standing behind me. Only when a bus came and I didn't move, I heard a commotion building behind me and only then did I realize that it was me who was the cause of this commotion. A queue had formed behind me in just a few minutes. Some discipline, eh!" finally concluded Brig CAT Menon.

"If every Indian followed this code of civic sense strictly, India would be a different country. But then" he continued "the population in India is so much that it is a Herculean task to provide education to all. It is education that makes a man think rationally. When India got her Independence in 1947 what was the situation then? It was utter chaos with the British having taken away whatever they could, leaving this country in doldrums. It has taken us about 60 years to correct this situation and progress both economically and socially. Today, the whole world looks to us for development, thanks to the software industry progressing at exponential speeds. Throwing your garbage in the street instead of putting it in a plastic cover and leaving it at your gate for the garbage collector to pick it up, jumping the queue at a super market cash counter by thrusting your hand from behind in the process knocking on someone's head. Why this sort of behavior? Can't you be patient?" Brig Menon paused to take a sip of water. "Like this there are plenty of situations you would come across everyday, where a little patience can do the trick."

A couple of days later, as soon as Arti had finished her interview successfully, a brilliant idea crossed Brig Menon's mind. He had always believed that it is better to teach his children and the Army Officers' children certain formalities and etiquettes that are to be followed in everyday life when they come across different situations.

He discussed with his Commanding Officer, if he along with 2 other officers could take a week long session, one and a half hours each day for 5 days, in the afternoons between 4 and 5.30 on etiquette. The participants can be any young officer, senior officers' children between the age of 16 and 25 years. The objective was to make them better people both in the civil and army life.

Approval was immediately granted by their Commanding Officer.

Brig Menon himself had travelled widely both in India and abroad and excelled in his discipline. He was the military Attaché in the Indian Embassy, in Washington, USA for a year followed by another stint in Paris. Earlier, he had attended a course at The Royal Military Academy in Scotland. He had also traveled to Germany and Vienna with his family.

This sort of training had never been attempted in the past. They did not want this delayed and wanted it as soon as possible . . . It also suited Rohit and Arti as they had about 2 weeks' time before they reported for work.

Preparations commenced at express speed and by the end of the day they had prepared circulars announcing the commencement of this course from the following Wednesday. Interested aspirants could register before Wednesday 12 noon.

The faculty met in Brig Menon's house that evening and prepared the syllabus and promised to complete it by the next evening.

The course was to start that same afternoon from 3 O'clock sharp. The response was good with a record registration of 30 students. Admissions were capped at the same number.

The session started at 3 pm sharp with a brief introduction by Brig CAT Menon explaining the need for this course and without wasting time he started.

Notebooks and pencils were distributed and participants were encouraged to take down notes.

Brig CAT Menon started with the discipline needed at home including table manners to be followed at home and outside. He also touched upon how parents should bring up their children patiently teaching them good manners and discipline.

"One major lack of discipline shown by many" continued Brig Menon, "is the habit of leaving the gate of a bungalow open after you have gone in or out. How long does it take to close the gate? Have they realized the inconvenience being caused to the inmates? A thief could stealthily walk in. A cow or a buffalo could walk in and feast in the garden. Stray dogs could come in and when confronted could bite someone. It is polite to close the door behind you when you enter a room.

Another bad habit is parking your car(s) or two wheeler(s) in front of the gate or on the road causing inconvenience to others. Don't they care for others, these self—centered people? They look at only at their convenience.

One must introspect. How would you feel if these were to happen to you? What would be your reactions? Well, these are the feelings of others also. Try and avoid causing inconvenience to others. They are also your fellow beings and have fundamental rights as much as you do. Live and let live." finally concluded Brig Menon.

"Thank you for listening patiently and Good night."

Driving

During the next few days Brig Menon was busy preparing his lectures. He was closeted in his study every morning for about an hour.

When the classes began he decided to talk on the discipline required while driving.

"Many drivers, especially the ones who are way down the queue at a traffic light, start honking as soon as the light turns green." They do this deliberately to harass the drivers in front who can start moving only when the others in front of them start moving. It is not possible for all the vehicles to start together. It is not a car race. They do not show any patience. The elderly drivers can have a heart attack when they are harassed and put under pressure. This happens by and large only in India and not in any developed or other developing countries. One habit among the drivers, particularly the heavy vehicle drivers and taxi drivers is the flashing of headlights or on "bright" or "high beam" to bulldoze their way past another vehicle dazzling the oncoming drivers, which is highly dangerous. I understand flashing of lights mean different things in different countries. However, in India it is certainly not a friendly signal." continued Brig Menon.

"It is the police who are to blame for this, largely. The traffic police are busy catching auto-rickshaw drivers without uniform, two wheelers without pollution control test certificate or helmet to name a few. Not so long ago, I was fined by the traffic police for not having a "pollution free" certificate despite driving a non polluting vehicle as declared by the manufacturers. They miss the woods for the trees. They do not book traffic offenders, the ones that jump the traffic light, the ones who honk in a 'no horn' area, the lane switchers, the ones who park ahead of the stop line and so on.

They do not try to prevent accidents. They perform post mortems. The objective of giving these examples is to have a little consideration **for** others around you. Have you ever imagined that you could also be in a similar situation at some point in time?"

"How would you feel if you are holding the wrong end of the stick."

"Lane discipline is virtually absent. Very often you can see some cars and motor bikes driving at break neck speeds, switching lanes without signaling. This is very dangerous. On top of this some of them use their mobile phones while driving. Although this is forbidden, the traffic police do not enforce this law strictly. One can play the blame game but when are you going to learn? Don't you think it is better to learn through others' mistakes rather than learn the hard way?"

Art of listening

"One other important area," continued Brig CAT Menon "is the **Art of listening**. Understanding this art is very vital. One often comes across people who do not have the patience to listen.

This is a very valuable skill. It is an art. If you do not have it please acquire it or cultivate it. It is nice to be a good listener rather than putting the cart before the horse. There is another old saying which states 'It is better to remain silent and be considered a fool rather than open your mouth and confirm it.' There are many a time, I am sure, you might wanted to put your foot in your mouth. Be patient. Patience is the mother of all virtues. Listening carefully gives you the time to think of an appropriate reply. In a conversation one has to listen while the other talks. If both talk at the same time what happens? You can imagine the confusion it would create.

- Many a time, it can be noticed that when 3 or 4 people are standing and talking, let's say, for example, in a party, you would find someone coming into a gathering and joining the conversation. So far so good. Very soon he would move and stand in front of you and start talking to the person in front of you completely disregarding your presence. This is a very bad habit and very annoying. This is done, at times unwittingly and at times deliberately. You would also find them interrupting the conversation without a hint of guilt of having barged in. They like to be heard. They do not like to listen unless compelled. These are traits of conceit and selfishness. Taking others for granted. It is unfair to do so.

It was the end of the session that day and there were a few clarifications sought.

On day following day the Brigadier spoke about the Dressing etiquette and the dining etiquette which he had discussed in detail with his family. He emphasized the need to make these etiquettes your second nature which can be done only with regular practice. He said dressing for a party or a wedding reception is quite different from dressing to office or for an interview. To a wedding reception women can really afford to put on all the paint they want but they should remember to check in the mirror to see how they look before leaving. Some would look monstrous while some would look over painted as if they were going for a film shooting. Please remember, people will ridicule you and laugh behind your back if you are dressed like a clown while they would secretly admire you if you have a sense of dressing that is simple and smart . . .

Day two again ended with the participants asking clarifications of all sorts and the Brigadier and his colleague Colonel Nayak answered them to the best of their abilities. The participants wanted printed notes to be circulated so that they can use it as a ready reckoner.

When it was time to start the session on day three Brig CAT Menon said, "Today I am going to talk about some very important topics on Business Etiquette, Conversation building, introductions during business meetings, etc. It would be incomplete if I do not touch upon some of the business and office etiquettes. I will also touch upon presentation skills besides travel and social etiquettes."

Office Etiquettes

- The most commonly found practice among people in the office is to talk loudly on the telephone which sometimes gets very animated resulting in flying debris. If not the debris, the loud talk disturbs others besides letting out confidential information inadvertently.

- Learn to talk softly and in a composed manner. It displays confidence and a firm head on your shoulders. There should be no emotional outbursts as far as possible. It also keeps your blood pressure under check.

- Another common practice is to throw things around especially paper, all over the place. I may be exaggerating but you can see an unclean office many a time. This should be avoided at all costs.

- A clean environment is so pleasing for everybody. Nowadays, it is a paperless office in most places. In such an environment communication becomes easier and faster.

- Remember . . . . cleanliness is next to Godliness. This is what we are taught in school."

"Whew, this was a long session." thought Big CAT Menon. "Ladies and Gentlemen, please give me another 5 to 6 minutes of your time. I would like to add something that most of you are aware of but some of you may not be following. The thing that comes to my mind is the habit of interrupting when someone is talking. Some people, who perhaps like to hear their voice and no one else's, interrupt without any warning. It would be courteous if you were to say "excuse me" and after the speaker has stopped and looked at you, only then should you start talking. To make matters worse he stands in front of you, between the person you are talking to and you. This is sheer bad manners resulting out of poor upbringing and a lack of concern for others."

Travel Etiquette and Communication

B rig CAT Menon decided to give a 5 minute break as he knew that the topic of the day would spill over the next 2 hours.

"Ladies and Gentlemen," continued Brig CAT Menon after the break, "please pay very close attention to what I am going to talk for the next hour or so. It is all the more important to people who travel frequently, particularly abroad."

"People travel both within India and outside," continued CAT Menon. "Let us talk of the domestic traveler whether it be by rail or air, there is a large element of impatience shown by them. At the starting station, let's say for example, you have reached the station well in advance and the train was just steaming into the platform. As soon as the train stops, there is a mad rush to enter the train despite having a valid reservation and plenty of time for the train to depart. I don't understand this, do you?" he enquired. Having got in, there is a scramble to find space to keep your baggage. Luckily, these days, people travel with minimal luggage. Then it is all quiet and people look around and wonder when the train is going to start.

Even at the airport, after you have checked in and cleared security when the bus comes to take you to the aircraft there is a mad rush to get in and find a place to sit down. The trip to the aircraft is going to last five minutes at the most. Yet they show impatience. We have to learn to be patient. Things would be much easier".

"Coming to international travel," continued Brig Menon after pausing to take a sip of water, "it is worse at times. Having gone through all the check in formalities and boarded the aircraft after a long wait due to bad weather, the passengers' patience are at their wits end. As soon as they have settled down they want a drink of whisky or whatever, they don't actually care, as most airlines offer free drinks on board. There is a scramble for it and the hostesses tend to lose patience. They announce that drinks would be served only after takeoff. Grumbles follow but there is no choice. As soon as the aircraft takes off and the 'fasten your seatbelt' sign goes off the passengers are ready for their free drinks. They gulp down a couple of them and demand more. Soon they protest the refusal of the cabin crew until one of them complains to the Captain of the flight and he makes an announcement that dinner or lunch, as the case may be, would be served and lights would be switched off soon after. He wishes them a pleasant flight and signs off. In-flight courtesies are essential. After all there are other passengers who are traveling and they have as much rights as you have. The cabin crew is doing its duty. Just be quiet and normal. If you give respect it would be reciprocated.

- While travelling abroad it would be better to know different English accents, expressions, habits and customs as much as possible as it helps you adapt much faster. First of all, you would be able to understand what they are saying. 'When in Rome be a Roman' it is said. You would have no choice but to follow their customs and habits.

- When it comes to speaking English, accent is an important aspect which we as Indians do not pay much attention to. Each state in India has more or less a distinct accent. It is more of Indian English or "Hinglish" which is a mixture of Hindi and English. The South criticizes the North, the West criticizes the East and so on but none of them follow either the American accent or the British accent. English is their language and is best spoken their way. It is here that we lose out to the Filipinos, the Chinese or the Japanese or even some of the Western non-English speaking countries. When they are taught English, there is a great emphasis on the accent. It helps a great deal, especially these days when medical transcription is a big opportunity to do business as well as for jobs. Take the Keralites, for instance, the state with the highest literacy rate. However, their pronunciation is not appropriate and because of this they have missed out on a lot of employment opportunities by the multinationals in the software industry. They have realized this and have started taking corrective actions." continued CAT Menon." "Today, believe you me, some of the finest candidates come from this state."

- After a pause to drink water, Brig Menon continued. "It is the politicians who are largely to blame for this. The education pattern is not need-based but knowledge oriented. Knowledge alone is not enough. There should be an opportunity to exercise it. One must realize, that command over the language, at least the spoken one, is necessary to communicate effectively and only if you can communicate effectively will you be listened to. Only when you are listened to will you be recognized. It is vital that children, in their formative stage, are taught the correct usage of

English. We are not Japan or China or Germany where the native tongue is advanced enough to have literature in the medical, engineering and the commercial fields. Even they have found the need to learn English the proper way. It is important in almost all fields be it education, medicine, engineering **or** entertainment, you cannot do without English."

- "Nowadays a lot of slang is used in English. Many words are American, obviously spread from their movies, books and not to forget the television. There are many Indians in the US, who are software engineers, doctors, nurses, business people and in the scientific community. Admissions for higher studies to the US have also become easier but, remember, one has to pass an English proficiency test (*TOEFL . . . Test of English as a Foreign Language*) / *IELTS (International English Language Testing Services)* for getting admission to any university in the US." said Brig CAT Menon.

- It is also an easy language to learn. In fact, it is one of the largest used languages worldwide. It is one of the national languages of our country and also the most commonly used, particularly in the metros. Across the world, English is taught largely in American accent, except, of course in England, mainly because of the influence the US has in commerce and in movies besides in the software industry. It has therefore become important that focus should be on the American accent because of the opportunities this country offers to the world. Take, for example, the field of medicine. Most of the research and development are in the US. Opportunities for nurses are the highest from this country. Medical transcription from the US is a tremendous Business opportunity. Here it is vital that you know the American accent very well because it is a dictated report of a surgery by the surgeon or a physician's report after examining a patient. The job of the Medical Transcriptionist is to type the reports and send it back to where it came from in the shortest possible time so that when the doctor comes on his next round of examinations the report is made available. If the accent is misunderstood then the reports would go wrong. The follow up action would go wrong and the patients' life would be in danger. Similarly, when the nurses get instructions from the doctors' for follow up and if the instructions are not understood correctly, the patient would be wrongly treated. Haven't we heard of many cases where wrong treatment has caused the loss of lives or the patient has become an invalid?"

Day 3 ended with the participants looking quite tired. A lot of information has been pumped into them. Brig Menon, with the permission of the audience, took a further 10 minutes to complete the telephone courtesies.

Tipping is another important aspect which we will talk about in due course.

Tipping like a Gentleman

"Tipping really is an art form and when you're giving your tip you want to be as discrete and gentlemanly as possible." started Brig Menon. "Hand over the tip with your palm facing down and shake hands with the person you are tipping, simultaneously placing the money in their hand. What you want to avoid doing is waving the money around and making a big deal of it. You'll look like an idiot to start with and if that isn't enough, you're going to make the person receiving the tip feel uncomfortable because, believe it or not, you're coming across like a condescending jerk. You're not throwing a treat for Fido here. So how do you figure out how much to tip? Well the truth is there are no tipping rules per se, however there are guidelines which suggest how much is appropriate to give. Let's investigate.

The restaurant waiter/waitress

This is the one that causes most debate because there is no hard and fast rule. It is also made even more difficult by waiting staff who have lost sight of the fact that a tip is a gratuity and is not **mandatory.** As a guideline though, I'd say you can safely use the following suggestions.

Self-serve/Buffet restaurant—*10-12%*. If the service was fantastic, you could up this to *15%*.

A la carte restaurant—*15%*. Again, you could up this by a few points if the **waiter** worked particularly hard or went out of **his** way to help you.

A 4-star restaurant—You'll want to tip the maitre d' as you're being seated, particularly if you're a regular and he/she goes out of their way to reserve you a table or get a table when the restaurant is busy. The standard tip here is anywhere from Rs 50/-.to Rs 100/-.

For the service of the meal itself, I'd recommend a tip of around *15% to 20%* of the billed amount. Some restaurants include 10% of the billed amount, in the bill. In such a situation a minimum tip of Rs 50/—would do, ie, if you want to. Don't forget to tip the wine steward (*a few rupees* per bottle of wine) and/or the coat check attendant (Rs 25 or $5 for a couple of coats).

Taxi driver

Unless you want to annoy the Travis Bickle-esque taxi driver by stiffing him on a tip you'd better go ahead and give *15%* of the fare.

Hair Dressing

You want to make sure your hair looks as good as possible and tipping will ensure that your hair stylist gives you a polished cut. They'll also be more likely to look after you next time you visit too (I've been given a free **hair** colour **once** for simply tipping well). An acceptable amount is somewhere in the region of *10-15%* of the cost.

Hotel staff

There are a number of staff members at the hotel that can make your stay very pleasant or a living nightmare depending on how you tip them. Here's who you should tip and how much to give them:

Chambermaid—*$5 or Rs 25* per night of stay. That is, if you want clean sheets, towels and plenty of toilet rolls.

Room service waiter—Again this is the standard 10% to *15% of the bill.*

Bellhop—If you let the bellhop carry your bags up to your room and show you around **the** room, tip them around *Rs.10-15* for their efforts.

The Casino (for overseas travelers)

If you're going for a night out at the casino, you better be prepared to tip. Of course if you're a professional gambler (or just extremely lucky) you'll be able to tip from your winnings.

Blackjack dealer—*$5 chip* (or more) per session. It's also common place in casinos for the players to place a small side bet for the dealers. You can agree the amount with other players but a *$1 chip* is usually sufficient.

Craps dealer—Those craps dealers love the action as much as you. It's common to place up to a *10%* side bet for the dealer.

Poker dealer—*$5* per session. Winners usually tip at least *$10* and sometimes as much as *10%* on bigger wins.

Drink waitresses—*$1 chip* per drink.

Parking attendant

You don't want some juvenile attendant ruining your prized Mercedes because you didn't tip the lad, do you? On second thoughts, why would you let a juvenile attendant park your prized Mercedes unless you're asking for trouble?

You should tip, at the very least *Rs 50 (additional Rs 10 if they help with your luggage,)* but I would tip a little extra to get a better level of service. Oh, that reminds me, I always check the mileage of the car before handing it over to a parking attendant!

But what if I don't want to give a tip?

There are certain occasions where you feel unjustified to give out a tip, but let me tell you why you should.

The food was terrible.

If the food was terrible, then complain to the manager *(you might get a discount on the bill)* but don't take away the tip from the waiting staff because you're punishing them for someone else's mistake. Chances are they worked very hard for you and not to reward them would be unfavorable.

The service was below par.

If the service was below par then you should tip at a lower rate than normal. Usually, I'd speak to the waiter I'm tipping and politely explain the reasons for the lower tip. Just make sure you've eaten all your food before you tell them so!

You are a stingy and grumpy old man.

So you don't want to tip. Why not? You're rewarding someone for doing good work. How would you feel if your boss decided to not give you the pay raise you've been expecting or taking your bonus away from you just because he felt like it? As the old saying goes, "Treat other people the way you expect others to treat you."

Telephone Courtesies

Many people dial a number and ask on the phone "who is speaking" without identifying themselves. This is bad manners. How would you feel if your telephone rings and when you answer you are greeted with a similar question? As a caller, it is good manners or etiquette that you identify yourself and ask for the person you want to speak to by name. This courtesy applies both for the land and the mobile telephones, whether you are at work or at home. Children must be taught this. While in office you have to either mention your name when you lift the receiver or you should mention the company's name. It makes a world of a difference if you were to use the word "please" while conversing on phone and even while talking to your colleagues or subordinates. The response you get will be surprising. It leaves an aura of pleasantness. In fact, if you are smiling during a conversation on the phone, the person at the other end can feel it. If another phone rings while you are on the first phone, then it is courtesy that you ask the first caller to hold on for a while when you find out who the second caller is and depending on the importance of the call, disconnect one of the phones after excusing yourself but promising to call back. Whenever you are free, you must return that call or else you are being discourteous while keeping that caller in suspense."

"I didn't realize that etiquette included all these. I thought it was just the usual courtesies one expressed in everyday life but God, there is more to it. I need to learn all these as it will be useful while travelling abroad." said Anit, one of the participants.

"We have two more days to go and I hope to at least touch upon the other important aspects like Presentation skills, ordering of food in the restaurant, etc. If one were to go in detail then this would be a 6 month course including practicals." With these words Brig Menon ended the day. The session had lasted more than two hours.

Presentation Skills

It was Day 4 of the Etiquette classes and Brig Menon started the day with a brief revision of the previous three days' lessons. "I hope you are reading the previous day's notes. It would help you to remember them." started Brig Menon. The hall looked full and the Brigadier realized there were an additional twenty or so students in that day's class. "Interesting!" thought Brig CAT Menon.

- "Today we would take a look at Presentation skills." said Brig CAT Menon. "First of all it is important to know the subject you are planning to present, thoroughly.

- It would help if the audience are strangers as you can expect fewer questions but if it is a small known audience you have to be well prepared as you can expect tricky questions from them. There are various ways of making a presentation. Some are colorful with background music to add a little glamour, some are prerecorded and some are sharp and simple where the presenter makes his or her point orally during the presentation. While it is essential to have a thorough knowledge of the computer and the various options in terms of effects, styles, etc it offers, it is also important to concise the contents to points so that the visual aspects are just right and the oral presentation does the rest. Please remember that at the end of the presentation the audience would shoot questions at you and you should be prepared to answer them without batting an eyelid.

While preparing for a presentation, one must know

- The Objective
- The Subject matter
- Required Statistics
- Time allotted and
- How to prepare
- Preparation is the key to success. The presentation should be precise and to the point. Choice and clarity of the words should be appropriate. By choosing the right type of font and the right size to make it easier for the audience to sit up and listen. It should have the right amount of charts and graphs to convey complete information. These graphics should be explained briefly leaving

room for questions for you to answer and clarify. The color combination is also important to give your presentation a pleasing look. While all these are important, it is necessary to practice the presentation well at home to make it interesting and avoid embarrassment should you fumble while answering questions. As for the presenter, he or she must be well groomed and formally dressed to give an air of seriousness. Please do not smoke during the presentation as it is an indication of nervousness and being curt. Do not overact or use very complicated words while talking. If you are speaking in English or for that matter in any language please ensure that you speak calmly, clearly and slowly. Give an ear to the audience when they interrupt you. You could either clarify their queries then and there, or request them to keep their questions for the end to be answered during the question hour.

- Presentations are usually made directly from the laptop using a videoscope which comes as an attachment.

- Sometimes it is done on an Acetate which is a plastic sheet using a pen having a non deletable ink. *(these are available in any stationery shop in all basic colors)*. Here the points are hand written or printed and the presenter explains whatever is shown. These sheets are projected onto a screen using a projector. "

Having completed the session on Presentations let us move on to another interesting topic which is the art of conversation. I will give you a five minute break. Please be back in your places on time," said Brig CAT Menon.

Five minutes down the line and all the participants were back in their seats and were eagerly looking forward to go to the next topic.

The Art of Conversation

"**G**ood evening Ladies and Gentlemen for the second time today. We will now talk about different types of conversation." He began.

"When I say 'conversation' I mean the process of talking between friends, colleagues, family members . . . and so on. With each of these sets of people mentioned above, the styles of speaking vary although the topics may be the same. The confidence level shown by the speaker also would vary from the relaxed to the formal. While the formal may also be relaxed there is an element of difference in the choice of words and the accent besides the speed and tone. Greater the knowledge, greater is the confidence level.

The formalities observed vary between a dialogue with your boss and the one with your colleagues or friends. It all depends upon the upbringing and command over the language, in this case English. It is absolutely necessary to modulate your voice depending on whether you are making a presentation or introducing a chief guest at a function or giving a vote of thanks or speaking at a function as the main speaker. I am not advocating that everyone follow one standard style and speak like robots. Listen to the American or the British speak or for that matter the Australian. All of them carry the accent of their country. It is only the accent that varies. Unlike the English spoken by an Indian from the South vis—a—vis one from the North or East or West. It is not only that the accent that varies but the use of the language itself.

Everyone has an ability to speak but speaking well varies from person to person. Some feel very much at home while speaking to an audience while many others feel extremely shy and maybe at a loss for words. It is the practice and the will to succeed that brings out the best in a person. There should be a smooth flow of words, well punctuated and at a speed which can be understood and clear to all. The secret of making a talk interesting is to choose simple words, interspersing your speech with live examples, adding a little humour here and there and most of all presenting a relaxed and confident self. Gestures should be minimal and not wild so as to knock the microphone down. Your emotions should be easy and controlled so as not to go to the extremes.

There are certain etiquettes **to** be followed while delivering speeches. Please do not forget the names of the people on the dais and do not forget to acknowledge their presence. A well prepared speech is a well delivered speech. However much an expert you may be, it is worthwhile rehearsing a couple of times before you leave your home or office. It would be advisable to keep a small note in your palm which is well hidden. This gives you the confidence and to speak without interruption because you know that you can always refer to the note if there is a need.

Coming to the dress that is to be worn, it depends on the occasion but it is always better to be formally dressed. It may not matter whether you wear a suit or not but a well fitting, neat dress is essential. It also looks good and pleasing.

An important aspect to be followed when talking among your friends is to talk in the same language that is understood by all in that group. Indians particularly, since they come from different states where different languages are spoken, tend to speak in their mother tongue if there is another person from the same region in the group. This is impolite as the others would feel left out or feel you are talking something ill about them which you do not want them to hear, when you speak in your mother tongue. It is not good manners. Similarly, please keep your emotions in check and do not speak loudly to make yourself heard. Please be patient and await your turn. Do not barge into the conversation or interrupt when another person is speaking. These things are important and I suggest that you practice them consciously.

When you are in a public place like a restaurant or an airport or a railway station where there are other noises which interrupt your talking it is better to be as close as possible to the person with whom you want to speak and speak in a tone just loud enough to be heard by that person.

While speaking to elders please show respect for their age. Remember, one day you too would reach that age and would not like to be ridiculed by youngsters. It is a practice in India that you refer to a person older to you as your brother or an uncle if he is very much older than you. Similarly, you would address a lady who is older than you as your sister and an elderly lady as your aunt. This showing of respect to our elders is taught in the ancient Hindu scriptures.

However, sometimes nowadays, these kinds of courtesies seem to be taking a back seat. It would not be out of place to mention that many Americans envy the togetherness that is present in India which is absent among them. A family remains together facing and sharing all the good times and the bad. They do not split up at a drop of a hat as it happens in the west and calling these individual rights. The 'so what' attitude would spell disaster. Aping the west and taking their good points is wise but aping them as a whole would spell doom. No wonder the Indian Spiritual Gurus find listeners in the West before they come to India so that they get recognition.

Socializing Skills

It does not require any special skills to socialize. One has to apply common sense when approaching strangers to start a conversation. A simple greeting of a "Hello" or "Hi" is good enough. To start with you have to introduce yourself and say a few words about yourself, short enough to give them a bird's eye view of yourself and not a long drawn one so as to bore them. Having done this, give them a chance to talk about themselves. Be a good listener and lo and behold! you have already struck a conversation. Move around in the crowd greeting people, pause if you find an interesting person to carry on a conversation and finally settle down with a group where you are welcome and you are comfortable. Before you realize you'll find that you have become friends.

At the outset one has to be an open person, an extrovert. Listening is an art you have to master and one should speak only when you are addressed. Never butt in. If you need to interrupt, please seek permission like 'May I say something please?' Excuse me", or draw attention to the speaker by looking at him with a 'wanting to talk look'. Another art one should develop is the art of listening carefully and putting questions to the speaker as if you know the answer and sure enough, the speaker will answer it. In the process you have got your answer and doubts clarified. If you get stuck when asking a question or the speaker realizes that you do not know the answer to his query, you should be smart enough to wriggle out of the situation. Please remember, there is no prescription for this. You have to be street smart and learn as you go along. No Business School or for that matter, no course or school teaches you these finer aspects of life as a subject. One has to be a good observer and notice things that are around you. It is not enough if you look. You have to see it. There are various techniques to teach you these aspects of life. However, it is too long a topic to discuss here.

Among the modern generation it is common to offer a drink, be it alcohol or a soft drink, to the guests. Please specify your preference and say a 'Thank you' after you have taken it. Please make it a point to say a 'Thank you' whenever anybody does something good to you like offer a book or a drink or invites you over to watch a movie, etc. If you do not want to accept it please say, "No, Thank you". Please leave your glass or plate at the appropriate place without making a mess. All these small things you do get noticed by your hosts or your seniors and goes a long way in your progress in life or career. As mentioned earlier you have to be appropriately dressed for the occasion.

Dress smartly, be it formal or casual. If casual please ensure your dress is not gaudy or ill fitting. Make sure your footwear is neat and polished. In many Indian homes, footwear is not worn inside the homes. In such places remove your footwear and keep it neatly outside wherever there is a provision. Finally, I would like to add that it is your power of observation and assimilation of the good things while discarding the bad or unwanted that will get you noticed and bring you success." concluded Brig CAT Menon.

Time Management

"Let me take you through one of the most important aspects of everyday life Time Management!" said Brig CAT Menon. "Many of us tend to take each other for granted which is not correct. One of the most commonly heard complaint is,.'I don't have the time' 'I am busy!' If only you were disciplined enough you would have all the time in the world to do what you want." continued Brig Menon. "One has to plan one's daily activities and adhere to it. You have to pass on this message down the line and even up in your work atmosphere. It is only in India that people complain about lack of time. The IST is humorously called 'Indian Stretchable Time'. Why should this happen? It is nothing but the lack of proper planning, as I said earlier. At the cost of repetition, one has to strictly follow one's plans. One can speak volumes on this topic as it is the most spoken about topic in the Management world. The higher you go in the hierarchy more the pressure you are in and if you cannot manage your time, you may not last there very long. In other words, you are capable of managing your time provided there is a Damocles sword hanging over your head". Brig Menon paused to have a sip of water.

"You may be wondering why I am talking of Time Management in a session on etiquette. It is said 'Time and Tide wait for no man'. To elucidate this, if you had to catch a flight at the city airport or board a train at the city railway station and you have your office at a place quite far away, if you don't leave your office well in advance, considering the city traffic, chances are you are going to miss your flight or train if you are late. They are not going to wait for your arrival. In such cases, you ensure you are at the airport or railway station well in time. The point is, why don't all of you apply the same rule at all times? It is not good to keep someone waiting for you. They also have their priorities.

In one of the companies I had worked we had a new Managing Director who had joined just a month ago. He was a stickler for timings and he had told his secretary that whenever anyone wanted to meet him she should give them a specific time and also to tell them to be there on the dot lest their appointment should stand cancelled. 'This' he had said 'would apply to everybody without exception.'

A few days later, our Sr VP (HR) had sought an appointment at a particular time and the meeting was to last for 15 minutes. For some reason he was late by about 5 minutes. When he entered the MD's office he was curtly told by the MD that since he was late by five minutes there would not be enough time left to discuss and therefore to seek a fresh appointment from his secretary and meet him the next week. That was the last time anybody was late in meeting him.

A commitment is a commitment. You have to be fair to the other person. Being an MD he has a lot more responsibilities and cannot afford to be lax in his work. People from within the company and outside come to meet him and he has no right to waste their time. They might have made other commitments. The moment you recognize this fact you would be a changed person.

Let me share with you an incident that happened to me in Chennai. While on a business tour of Sri Lanka I had met the Managing Director of a company called Keels which is Sri Lanka's largest importer of scotch whiskies and other liquor besides manufacturers of meat products and many other FMCG brands of cosmetics, etc. After having been shown around their factories and warehouses I had an hour long meeting with their MD and a couple of other Directors. As I was leaving, their MD said he would be travelling to the US and a few other countries starting two weeks from then and was scheduled to return to Colombo after visiting South Africa. Instead of going directly to Colombo he would like to take a deviation via Chennai where he could visit our factory and our Management before returning home. Mind you, this commitment was made more than a month ago. He had given me his flight details and where he would be staying in Chennai. He was to come to our office at 6 in the morning and I was to pick him up and proceed to the factory about 200 kilometers away. The idea was to visit the factory in the morning and return after lunch to Chennai. Thereafter we could have a relaxed early dinner and he could go to bed so that he could catch a few hours sleep before leaving for Sri Lanka.

As luck would have, it I couldn't contact him the previous evening despite my best efforts till about midnight and thereafter in the morning from 4 a.m. I thought he had changed his program and had failed to keep me informed and went to office as usual at 8.45 am. The moment I parked my car the security came running to me to tell that a gentleman has been waiting since 6 in the morning and was furious. I quietly walked into my cabin wishing him 'Good Morning' as I sat down. His frustration broke down and he took off on me blaming me for being late etc. The office peon had already given him a cup of tea earlier. He again brought two cups of tea for us and two glasses of water. I did not interrupt him but listened patiently till he gave up after about 15 minutes. When he was through, I asked him if he had changed his schedule. He replied he had decided to stay with his friend at the last moment. When I told him I had spent the best part of the night in trying to locate him he said he had forgotten the diary in which he had my contact numbers. And therefore could not contact me. I knew I had a tight vice like grip on him then and he apologized for his outburst. In this case, I had a defense but in most cases one would look like a fool.

Brig Menon continued." While exporting various goods it is vital that you meet your schedule strictly as otherwise your consignment could be rejected as in the case of garments. If the garments do not reach the retail shelf before the season begins, your competitors would. You would cut a sorry figure besides losing your business. Besides, the commitments made by the importer down the line would be broken leaving the end user in a dilemma. Delays cannot be avoided but can be foreseen in most cases. In such cases it is better to reconfirm with your importer before dispatching them.

There are many examples I can give to drive home a point. A simple example is to make your wife wait at the restaurant and you go in late rather sheepishly. Can you imagine the outcome?

The moral of the story is never to take anyone for granted. Treat all of them equally. After all they are all your fellow human beings. Circumstances have made each one the way he or she is. None are to be blamed. One can talk on this subject for hours together giving a plethora of examples. Even the IIMs and many other Management institutes and also many companies spend as much as 2 days explaining the importance of Time Management. It shows how seriously it is being viewed in this professional business world. Many meetings, conferences, events, sports meets, travel and tours, medical decisions, etc take place around the world everyday. Just imagine for a moment if there are delays in these. Can you visualize the amount of confusion and damage it can create?

I can see the tired looks on your faces. I will stop for the day but I would like to have 2 hours tomorrow morning although it is a Sunday. I do not want to carry the sessions on to next week. I will bring some notes which you can refer. Having taken pains to do this much I do not want to fall at the 99th meter of a hundred meter race. One important topic on business etiquettes besides answering as many queries you may have. If you are here by 10 am sharp you will be free by noon. Do not miss this opportunity. You will not regret. Thanks and Good Night."

Sunday morning Brig CAT Menon woke up at 4 O'clock to prepare for the day's final session on etiquette he was taking. He had to prepare brief notes on the International travel etiquette and Business etiquette. The notes would be brief and he would explain only the salient features. Business etiquette and protocol is a vast subject by itself and books have been written on them. In view of its vast nature it is outside the scope of this session.

Brig Menon had just enough time to get ready after a quick breakfast and be at the venue for the final session. After all he couldn't be late as he would be setting a bad example even before his sessions are complete and nothing else can be more shameful than that. By five minutes past 10 am the entire class had assembled and was ready for the session to start.

"Good Morning and welcome to this final session." Brig Menon. "I am indeed very happy to see that All of you who had attended the earlier sessions have come and All of you are on time and ready within five minutes. It is like being battle ready. chuckled Brig Menon.

"I have prepared handouts which I request one of you to take photocopies and distribute. Meantime I will show you the acetates."

Business etiquettes

" It would be incomplete if I do not touch upon some of the business etiquettes." continued Brig Menon.

- Conversing inside office and outside is a very important aspect. The most commonly found practice among people in the office is to talk loudly which sometimes gets into animated actions resulting in flying debris. If not the debris, the loud talk disturbs others besides giving away confidential information inadvertently. I have already mentioned this earlier and I am repeating because of its importance.

- Learn to talk softly and in a composed manner. It exudes confidence and a firm head on your shoulders. There should be no emotional outbursts as far as possible. It also keeps your blood pressure under check.

Coming to the other aspects there are protocols and etiquettes in almost every business activity be it within countries or companies or ministries or federations, you name it, there are specially laid down etiquettes. When the President of a country visits us there is a certain protocol to be followed as to who would receive him and where would he be taken. When does he meet our President and so on. Similarly the business delegation accompanying him would meet at a set time with their counterparts in their respective countries, the topics for discussion are chosen before hand, etc. Likewise, International clubs like the Rotary, Lions, Free Masons, etc have a certain protocol.

I would suggest that those among you interested in understanding these protocols better can visit some leading library and locate a book and share it among others.

To summarise . . . .

1. International Business Etiquette:

Introductions and Exchanging Business Cards

Handshakes—**a firm handshake** make a powerful first impression

Eye Contact—sends powerful positive signals

Body Language and Gestures—discover country specific greetings

Professional Business Dress and Decorum—Suited for Success

2. Fine Dining Etiquette:

Formal Dinners

Handling different kinds of Food—Indian, Continental and Oriental.

Crockery and Cutlery—Cover setup and usage.

Napkin Etiquette

Dining Etiquette—Dos and don'ts

3. Communication:

Techno Etiquette (Speaker Phones, Voice Mail, Hand Phone)

Art of Small Talk—Striking Conversations, Taboo Topics, Pitch and tone of voice.

Verbal and non-verbal communication

Barriers to Effective Communications

Importance of Listening Skills

4. International Protocols: Forms of Address—Hierarchy,

Gender Dynamics—Door, Elevator, Workplace & Social

Networking and Mingling—Tips & Tricks to attract social friendship and development of business relations

Pre-meeting strategy and Preparation—Culture Demographics

Gifting—Acceptable & Unacceptable gifts

Protocols & Status

Receiving & Reciprocating.

5. Self discipline.

This is important as it reflects your character.

Days went by and turned into weeks and months. Rohit and Arti had joined their respective jobs and were doing well. Rohit was posted in Chennai and had opportunities to travel abroad a few times on short projects. He would recall what his father had taught him on etiquettes and was more than thankful many times. Arti, on the other hand was in Bangalore for a few months before she moved to Mumbai on another assignment with NDTV itself. They would be on video conference most of the time so that they were able to see each other and therefore did not miss each other's absence at home.

Arti was trying to get back to Bangalore and had requested the HR for a transfer. They said they would do so after one year. She was staying with an aunt in Mumbai. She was basically a quiet person and all her mother's training on self discipline had paid ample dividends. She would not poke her nose in unwanted matters at home. She would help her aunt in the kitchen and was pretty quiet at home so much so that her uncle and aunt had become very fond of her. They had a son who was in his school final and was preparing to become an engineer.

"Kamala" said Brig CAT Menon." You have been silent all this while whenever I was talking about etiquette."

"I was listening intently as I too wanted to learn. You had always ragged me of my country mannerisms. I wanted to make sure I don't make mistakes in a restaurant or anywhere for that matter. You know, I have been practicing eating with not only fork and spoon but also with chop sticks. Anyway, I am happy the kids have a father who is so concerned about their behavior that he has taken great pains to teach them and they are reaping the benefits now."

— — —

About the Author

 The author is a seasoned sales and marketing professional having travelled across the length and breadth of India and to a few foreign countries, in the course of his stint of over 25 years he had spent with two multinationals who were in the business of food and beverages, both alcoholic and non alcoholic. This book is a reflection of his experiences of the diverse culture, languages and food habits he was exposed to while interacting with people of different places who speak different languages. He graduated in English Literature from Madras Christian College in Madras (now known as Chennai). This college taught him the values of life and how to interact with people of different cultures. He also has a Post Graduate Diploma in Export Management

from The UK. He was also fond of penning poetry and short stories in his early days. Blessed with a sense of humor he is easy to get along and quick to make friends. Despite his age he still thinks young and that keeps him hale and hearty. This is his maiden attempt of a book.

www.ingramcontent.com/pod-product-compliance
Lightning Source LLC
Chambersburg PA
CBHW071354310526
45790CB00017B/631